THE ELEMENTS

Gold

Sarah Angliss

BENCHMARK BOOKS

MARSHALL CAVENDISH
NEW YORK

Benchmark Books
Marshall Cavendish Corporation
99 White Plains Road
Tarrytown, New York 10591-9001

Library of Congress Cataloging-in-Publication Data
Angliss, Sarah.
Gold / by Sarah Angliss.
p.   cm. — (The elements)
Includes index.
Summary: Explores the history of the precious metal gold and
explains its chemistry, how it reacts, its uses, and its importance
in our lives.
ISBN 0-7614-0887-8
1. Gold—Juvenile literature. [1. Gold.] I. Title.
II. Series: Elements (Benchmark Books)
QD181.A9A54 2000
669'.22—dc21   98-46800 CIP AC

Printed in Hong Kong

Picture credits
Corbis (UK) Ltd: 4, 18 *top*, 21.
Hulton Getty Picture Collection Ltd: 16.
Image Bank: 13, 15 *bottom*, 23, 26.
Image Select: 8, 12, 20.
John Bates: 10, 27 *bottom*.
Life File: 14.
Science Photo Library: 6, 7, 24, 25 *bottom*, 30.
Tony Stone Worldwide: 17 *top*, 17 *bottom*, 22.
World Gold Council: 5 *bottom*, 9, 11 *top*, 11*b*, 15*t*, 18*b*, 19*t*, 19*b*, 25*t*, 27*t*.

Series created by Brown Packaging Partworks
Designed by wda

Contents

What is gold?

Glistening bright yellow, gold is a heavy metal that is treasured in every country of the world.

Almost all metals have a characteristic luster (shininess)—that is, they reflect light in a mirror-like way. Gold is special because its luster never fades. That is because gold does not react with air, water, or any ordinary chemical. In other words, it doesn't corrode. Roman coins, masks from Ancient Egypt, decorated books from Persia, and other golden treasures from the ancient world shine as brilliantly now as they did the day they were made.

Inside the periodic table
Gold has the chemical symbol "Au." This is short for *aurum*, its name in Latin. In the periodic table, gold is positioned among the heavier transition metals—between platinum and mercury.

Inside the atom
Everything you can see is made up of microscopic particles called atoms. Inside each atom are even smaller particles: protons, neutrons, and electrons. Protons have a positive electrical charge, electrons have a negative electrical charge, and neutrons are neutral—they have no charge

Gold excites people's passions all over the world. The gold jewelry that people own is often among their most valued possessions.

at all. Protons and neutrons cluster together at the center, or nucleus, of the atom. The electrons spin around the nucleus in a series of shells.

Gold has an atomic number of 79, which means that it has 79 protons. The protons and neutrons combine to give an atom its mass. Gold has an atomic mass of 197, so it has 118 neutrons.

DID YOU KNOW?

A DESPERATE DASH

For thousands of years, people have hungered for gold—a desire that has cost many lives over the centuries. In the remains of the ruined city of Pompeii, Italy, archeologists discovered a dead body that was still clutching a bag of gold. Pompeii was destroyed in 79 c.e. by an eruption of the volcano Mount Vesuvius. This victim had probably grabbed his precious hoard as he tried to flee a city that was being engulfed by ash and poisonous fumes. It was a desperate dash for cash that proved fatal.

Melting pots

At room temperature, gold is solid. Gold melts at 1,943°F (1,062°C). It is often heated to this temperature so that it can be poured into molds (see page 18).

Gold is 19.3 times denser than water and three times denser than iron. Density means the mass of a substance that fills a

This astronaut's tether is his lifeline. It contains strands of gold that are guaranteed never to corrode. That means the tether should not snap and cause the astronaut to drift off into space.

given volume. It is usually measured in grams per cubic meter. So, one cubic meter of pure gold is 19.3 times heavier than one cubic meter of water. Imagine this: if you could just manage to lift a pail of water, you would need 19 friends to help you lift that pail if it were filled with gold instead.

Despite its great density, pure gold is soft enough to cut with a knife. This makes gold the perfect metal for intricate jewelry, artwork, and many industrial components.

This gold has been heated until it has melted and is now being poured so that it can be shaped into bars.

Where gold is found

Gold is extremely rare, which is one of the many reasons why we value it so highly. The proportion of Earth's crust that is made of gold is only five billionths.

As gold reacts with very few other chemicals, gold prospectors (people who search for gold) usually find it in its pure form. Occasionally, they come across gold that has combined with the metals bismuth, tellurium, or selenium.

Prospectors usually extract tiny crystals of gold, just a few millimeters in size. If they are very lucky, they may come across larger lumps of gold, known as nuggets. Gold is most often found in veins of a mineral called quartz. Sometimes it is discovered in loose chunks that pepper sand or gravel. These chunks are called placer deposits. They form when gold breaks free from rocks that have eroded (worn away). Running water, wind, or rain can erode rocks like this over millions of years.

The leading areas for goldmining include South Africa, Russia, the United States, Canada, Australia, Brazil, and China. The single most productive area is

Nuggets of gold like this are usually found in veins of the mineral quartz. Often, the gold is combined with another precious metal—silver.

Many prospectors have been misled by this very believable "lookalike" for gold. This is not a gold nugget but a sample of a mineral rich in iron rather than gold, commonly referred to as "fool's gold."

the Transvaal Province of South Africa, a country that now produces over a quarter of the world's annual gold production of 3,300 tons (3,000 tonnes).

Wealth beneath the waves

The oceans, which cover about three-quarters of Earth's surface, contain a much higher proportion of gold than the land. On average, one cubic foot (0.09 m³) of ocean is between 1,000 and 50,000 times more likely to contain gold than one cubic foot of Earth's crust.

Rich oceans but poor returns

Some 80 years ago, when people thought that there was more gold in seawater than there really is, German scientist Fritz Haber (1868–1934) was asked to find a way to extract the oceans' gold. His government wanted gold to pay the debts it had built up by the end of World War I (1914–1918). In fact, the proportion of gold in seawater is a mere 10 parts per trillion, so Haber succeeded only in showing that it would cost more to extract the gold than the gold would be worth.

Searching for gold

This old picture from the 1850s shows prospectors panning for gold during the California gold rush.

As traces of gold have been found and used by many ancient civilizations, it is impossible to say who first discovered this metal. But historic treasures and records that survive to this day show that many early peoples had a passion for gold. Cities have been founded and expeditions and wars started by people scrabbling for more of this precious metal.

Early gold prospectors, such as those in Persia and Ancient Egypt, probably panned for gold. Using river water, they would wash sand or gravel through a sieve. Any lumps of gold would be left behind in their sieve for them to collect.

Over the centuries, people have also developed the technology to dig gold out of solid rock. In the 16th century, the Spanish invaders of South America used slave labor to mine vast amounts of gold, changing the world economy forever. The population of states like Nevada

DID YOU KNOW?

THE FORTY-NINERS
Gold fever swept through California in 1849, the year after traces of the metal were discovered there. Over 100,000 "forty-niners" flooded into the area from Europe and the United States, hoping to find their fortune there.

The Rand district of the Transvaal, South Africa, is the largest goldmining area in the world. Until 1886, Johannesburg was a small village. Then gold digging began. Today, it is the main city in a country responsible for 29 percent of all of the world's gold production.

mushroomed in the 19th century as people rushed there to exploit newly discovered reserves of gold.

Gold mining is still big business, especially in South Africa. Today, gold prospectors use satellite technology and chemical rock analysis to search for new reserves. They can blast gold from rock using high-pressure water. They can even extract gold economically from low-grade ores (rocks that contain very small amounts of the metal). Gold can be dissolved from these rocks using the chemical potassium cyanide.

DID YOU KNOW?

A RIVETING STORY

The design of jeans may well have been perfected during the American gold rush. At that time, people needed hard-wearing trousers with pockets that could safely store nuggets of gold. People made their trousers out of rugged denim and put metal rivets around the pockets to ensure that their seams would not break.

DID YOU KNOW?

MINING SPACE

Some optimistic space scientists have suggested that we could mine asteroids for gold. It could cost many billions of dollars to capture and mine one of these lumps of rock in space, but the largest asteroids could contain vast quantities of gold and other precious metals.

Precious properties

GOLD FACTS

ACID REIGNS

Where other solvents (chemicals that dissolve other substances) fail, *aqua regia* (Latin for "royal water") succeeds. A deadly mixture of three parts nitric acid to one part hydrochloric acid, it is one of the few chemicals that can dissolve gold. It was used many centuries ago by alchemists—experimenters who wanted to turn ordinary metals, such as lead, into gold.

Gold catches our eye and is attractive to many people because it shines so brilliantly. People also like it because it is so rare and precious. But gold is valued for more than its scarcity and beauty. It has several other unusual properties that make it a perfect metal for many tasks.

Most metals, such as iron and copper, corrode over time. Corrosion happens when a metal combines with another element—usually the gas oxygen in the air—to form a compound that covers the metal's surface as a dull film. Gold objects never corrode. That is why they still look new even centuries after they were made. In fact, gold does not react in any way with water, air, and most acids, or with any other common substance.

Most metals suffer when exposed to the air and to the weather. Over the years, this bronze horse has become covered by a dull green-gray film of metal oxide. If the horse had been made of gold instead, it would still be glistening brightly.

Gold can be easily shaped—for example, into bracelets and bangles such as these.

Bend me, shape me

Pure gold is extremely malleable, which means that it is soft enough to bend or beat into many different shapes. You can beat a lump of gold with a hammer, for example, to turn it into a thin, flexible sheet of "gold leaf."

Gold is also very ductile. This means that it can be easily stretched into extremely fine wire, especially when first softened by heat.

Gold is an excellent thermal and electrical conductor—in other words, it lets heat and electricity flow through it very easily. Only silver and copper are more effective conductors of heat and electricity than gold.

Gold has these properties because of the way its atoms, the tiny particles that make it up, are arranged. Compared to most metals, gold has atoms that are bonded together very loosely. This means that they are able to slide past each other easily when only a tiny force is applied to them—for instance, when you try to bend or stretch a lump of gold.

With so many special properties, it is no wonder that gold can be put to so many different uses.

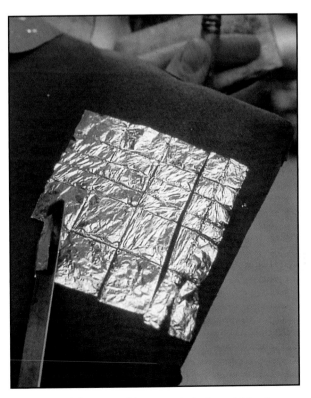

Less than $\frac{1}{250,000}$ in ($\frac{1}{10,000}$ mm) thick, gold leaf can be folded and torn as easily as paper.

DID YOU KNOW?

A LITTLE GOES A LONG WAY
A cube of gold the size of a plum could be beaten to form a sheet of gold leaf that could cover a tennis court, or it could be stretched to form a wire nearly 2 miles (3.2 km) long.

The gold standard

An assayer in 16th-century Venice, Italy, weighs a traveler's gold to find its value.

Gold's appearance never dulls, and its scarcity guarantees a high value. That is why people around the world rely on the ownership of gold as a good way to safeguard their wealth. It is therefore the ideal material to be used as money.

These days, when you travel to another country, you take some of the right currency (notes and coins) with you. But centuries ago, before there were formal ways to exchange currencies, travelers to foreign lands had to give something else in return for money or goods. So they took gold coins with them.

Almost every country had a use for gold, so anyone would be happy to receive gold coins from a traveler. Because gold does not corrode the coins would always be perfect, even if they had passed through several hands. By the beginning of the

DID YOU KNOW?

BURYING TREASURE

The single gold earring that sailors used to wear may well have been an early form of travel insurance. If a sailor died in a foreign land, his earring could be used to pay for his burial.

20th century, gold had become the standard way to compare the value of different currencies around the world.

From sterling silver to solid gold

Despite the obvious value of gold, nations first turned to silver as a standard to back up the value of their currency. For example, the English pound sterling was originally worth one pound of pure silver.

Britain adopted a gold standard in 1821, but the United States waited until the 1870s, when the discovery of gold greatly increased the supply. Under the gold standard, the amount of paper money a country issued had to be backed up by the same amount in gold reserves.

The United States kept to the gold standard until 1914, when World War I created a need for more paper money than gold supplies could support.

A new gold standard was set up and abandoned several times between 1928 and 1971, when the United States allowed its citizens to buy and sell gold in a free market.

Since then, the price of gold has varied from $200 per ounce to as much as $800 per ounce in times of economic uncertainty. Some countries have also resumed minting gold coins. These have a nominal face value but are always traded at higher prices based on the amount of gold they contain.

Hidden assets

Governments sometimes buy and sell billions of dollars worth of gold to change the value of their country's currency. But they rarely get to see the gold they buy: most of it is kept locked up in safe vaults around the world. In Switzerland, it is looked after by individuals mysteriously called the "gnomes of Zurich."

Stamped to show its authenticity, 45 percent of the world's gold is kept under lock and key in bank vaults as bars of gold bullion.

Alloys and films

Pure gold has countless uses, but gold is so expensive that manufacturers use it sparingly. A good and popular method of making a little gold go a long way is to mix it with other substances—usually other metals. Gold that is mixed with other substances has even more uses than pure gold. In art, in medicine, and in industry, people have found many reasons to add a touch of gold.

Getting the right mix

If you buy something made of gold, you'll be told its purity in *karats*. Pure gold, which is 24 karats (see page 26), is far too soft to make practical jewelry with. Most rings are made from gold that is 14 to 22 karats. These are alloys of gold and other metals, and they are much harder than pure gold. For example,

Stained-glass windows in cathedrals, such as this one at Ely in England, often include tiny specks of gold.

GOLD FACTS

GOOD MIXERS

Most gold jewelry is not made of pure 24-karat gold but of an alloy of gold with other metals. In the case of 18-karat gold, for example, the other metals make up one quarter of the alloy. The various alloys have different names, depending on the metals used. "Yellow gold" and "pink gold" contain different amounts of silver, copper, and zinc, while "white gold" contains palladium and copper and, sometimes, silver, nickel, or zinc.

---

an alloy of gold that is silvery in appearance is called "white gold." It is used in jewelry, dental work, and in minting some coins.

Gold can also be used in combination with glass, china, plastics, and even chemicals inside the body. The red and purple panes of cathedral windows, for example, are often made by adding specks of gold to molten glass.

A valuable property of gold is that, even in its pure form, it often needs only a tiny amount to be useful. Ordinary materials

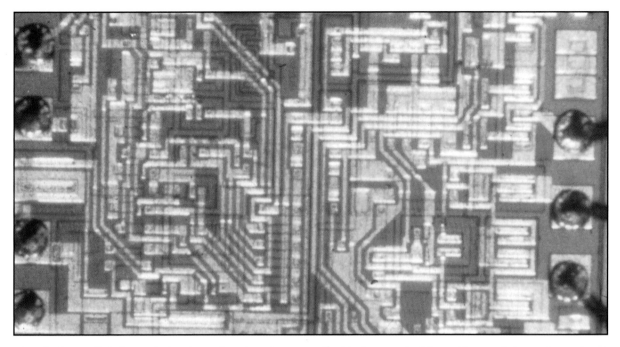

A technique called electroplating is used to deposit extremely thin layers of gold on objects to help protect and preserve them. Gold is electroplated onto such things as the circuit component shown above.

can be transformed by even the thinnest film of gold. For example, a film of gold less than a millionth of an inch thick applied to transparent plastic makes it a suitable material for a sun-shield. Used in a visor of a helmet, the gold film reflects the Sun's burning rays harmlessly away but still lets the wearer see through the plastic (see page 20).

Thin protective films of gold can be applied to metal surfaces by electrical means in a process called electroplating. The goldplated finishes on such things as surgical tools, knives and forks, and pieces of jewelry not only protect the items against corrosion, but also give them a more expensive look.

Gold coins are rarely made of pure gold these days. Usually, they are made of an alloy of gold with a cheaper metal such as nickel.

The art of gold

Reflecting light to create a beautiful luster, gold never loses its brilliance. As it is also easy to form gold into elaborate shapes, this precious metal has been used in sacred and important works of art for thousands of years.

At one time or another, people in every region of the world have used gold in their art. Some of the most acclaimed early goldsmiths were from Ancient Egypt, India, Greece, and South America. Ancient Egyptians, who associated glistening gold with their sun god, used it as decoration in life—and in death. Stunning examples of their goldwork were discovered when the tomb of King Tutankhamen (1370–1352 B.C.E.) was opened in 1922.

Like their ancient counterparts, more recent goldsmiths (people who work with gold), such as Russian Peter Carl Fabergé (1846–1920), have made intricate

This gold mask was sealed in the tomb of Egyptian king Tutankhamen 3,000 years ago. It amazed people with its brilliance when rediscovered in 1922.

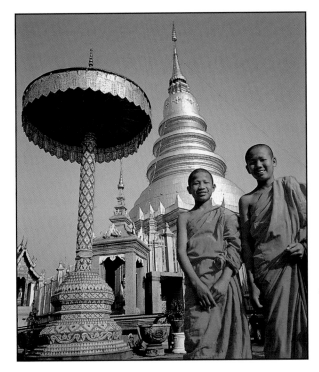

The roof of this pagoda in Thailand is covered with a thin layer of gold.

are often encrusted with gold. Gold is also used to decorate medals commemorating the highest bravery or achievement, for instance at the Olympic Games.

Golden weddings

For centuries, brides in many different cultures have been given rings or other jewelry made from gold. Traditionally, these golden gifts were also a form of financial insurance for women as they became part of a new family.

ornaments and jewels of gold. Working in the imperial Russian court at the end of the 19th century, Fabergé's famous creations included Easter eggs that were elaborately decorated with gold and precious stones.

Since gold is valuable, it is used to show people what we treasure or hold sacred. Around the world, holy temples and images

This Indian woman has a rich display of gold jewelry.

DID YOU KNOW?

GOLDEN VOICE

Eager to show off the wealth he had made through his music, rock 'n' roll legend Elvis Presley (1935–1977) bought himself a goldplated piano. This can still be seen at Graceland, his home in Memphis, Tennessee.

Working with gold

This initial letter "O" from an ancient Book of Psalms has been beautifully framed by gold leaf.

As pure gold is so easy to stretch into thin wire, to hammer, and to bend into different shapes, people have found many ways to work with it.

With a chisel, it is easy to engrave pure gold to produce solid figures or to make relief pictures. Scraps of gold that are chiseled away are not wasted. They can be melted together to form a new gold ingot.

Like most other metals, gold is also easy to cast. In other words, it can be melted, poured into a mold, then left to cool. Casting is an easy way to make many copies of the same metal object.

Since gold is so expensive, goldsmiths have found ingenious ways to make a little of it go a long way. They can beat it into gold leaf, for example. This can be used to cover a large area extremely thinly. Gold leaf decorates the pages of many of the world's most treasured handwritten books.

This gold medallion is being very finely engraved. You can tell how delicate the work is from the size of the engraver's fingernail at the top of the picture.

SOFT CENTERS

Hollow gold chains can be made by rolling a sheet of gold around a core of a more chemically reactive metal, such as copper or iron. The two metals are then drawn out together into a wire, with the gold on the outside, and shaped into chains. Finally, the finished chain is dipped in acid. This dissolves the inner core but leaves the gold intact. The advantage of hollow chains is that they are light in weight but still look heavy and impressive, and, of course, they use less gold than a solid chain would.

Gold is used to make gold teeth.

Gold can be pressed or plated onto silver. This creates vermeil, a slightly cheaper material that still looks and feels very much like solid gold.

Rolled gold is made of very thin sheets of gold pressed onto much cheaper metals, such as nickel or lead. It is often used to make inexpensive jewelry.

Filigree

Filigree is a technique for creating delicate effects in jewelry similar to lacework and intricate embroidery. Fine strands of gold wire are woven together and then rolled flat. Finally, they are twisted into coils, curls, spirals, and other attractive shapes.

These are some of the tools used by gold workers to shape gold and to beat it into delicate leaves.

WHAT GOLD IS USED FOR

In 1992, 3,100 tons (2,800 tonnes) of gold were mined, of which 80 percent was used to make jewelry. Of the remaining 20 percent, about half was turned into coins and ingots, and the rest was put to various industrial and medical uses.

Seeing with gold

Gold has its brilliant color because it reflects almost all of the yellow light that reaches it. These days scientists, as well as artists, put gold's reflective properties to good use.

An ultra-thin film of gold can reflect the Sun's rays. It is often applied to modern office-block windows, astronauts' visors, and the windows of aircraft cockpits to prevent the Sun from heating up or dazzling anyone inside.

The Apollo 11 *landing on the Moon in 1969. Astronaut Neil Armstrong can be seen reflected in the golden visor of fellow astronaut Buzz Aldrin.*

Night vision

Visible light, or sunlight, is a form of electromagnetic radiation, but it is not the only form of this radiation that gold can reflect. Gold also reflects almost all of the infrared radiation that reaches it. Infrared radiation, which is invisible to the naked eye, is the type of radiation that objects give off when they are hot.

At night, it may not be possible to see some objects, but if you have an infrared camera, you can find things by detecting the infrared radiation that they give off. For example, this is how night-time security cameras and burglar-alarm sensors work. The best night-vision cameras contain gold-covered infrared sensors, which enable them to detect even the tiniest traces of radiation.

Searching vision

Many space scientists study infrared images of the Universe. They use the images to learn more about the temperature of stars and the gases that make up planetary atmospheres. In fact, these images tell the story of the evolution of the Universe itself. To take these images, scientists need huge telescopes that are sensitive to infrared radiation. The mirrors of these telescopes are made of pure gold to ensure they reflect as much infrared radiation as possible.

Telescopes like the Keck telescope on Hawaii, which explore deep space, use goldplated mirrors. The picture shows one of the 36 segments of the mirror of the Keck telescope being serviced.

Gold connections

Airbags, like this one being tested on dummies, must work when needed, even after they have been packed for years inside a hot and dirty steering column. That is why their key circuit components are made of gold.

The world is undergoing a communications revolution. Along with plastic and silicon, gold is helping to change the way we keep in touch. Tiny amounts of gold are used inside almost every computer, television, video recorder, and modern telephone. So it is no surprise that the electronics industry uses more gold than any other industry.

The wires that connect circuits to the microchips at the heart of a computer, for example, are almost always made of gold (see page 15). This ensures that they conduct electricity easily and will also last for many years, even though they are amazingly thin. In fact, they are usually less than $\frac{1}{2,500}$ in ($\frac{1}{100}$ mm) thick.

A layer of gold over the delicate parts of a circuit can help to protect them and stop them from tarnishing over time. This is especially important in circuits where safety is critical: for example, the circuits that are used to fly a passenger aircraft or detonate an automobile's airbag system.

Gold in space

Communications satellites orbiting Earth relay telephone calls and TV programs around the world. If anything goes wrong with one of them, it would cost hundreds of millions of dollars to correct. That's why satellites have gold circuit components that are built to last. Satellites are also wrapped in a gold-covered film to protect them from harmful cosmic radiation (energy and particles that travel through space).

Golden explorer

Landing on the surface of Mars on July 4, 1997, the NASA *Pathfinder* probe sent stunning images of the planet back to Earth. Sheets of gold foil covered most of *Pathfinder*'s body to reflect the powerful rays of the Sun. *Pathfinder* also had many circuit components made of gold, as NASA scientists wanted to be sure it would work when it reached its destination.

Satellites such as this one are protected from the radiation in space by a film of gold.

Healing with gold

Gold reacts with very few chemicals, and so it is safe to use inside the body. For this reason, gold is being used more than ever to treat diseases and to investigate their causes.

For thousands of years, people who noticed gold's special properties have wondered if it has healing powers too. In Europe, for example, gold has been used as a popular remedy for ulcers and the joint disease arthritis. Over the past 150 years, scientists have looked closely at gold's healing properties, and they have devised new cures that use gold.

For over 100 years, medical researchers have known that compounds containing gold can stop the growth of some bacteria (microscopic creatures that can cause illness and disease), including the bacteria that cause the deadly disease tuberculosis (TB). Now researchers are investigating gold's ability to fight another deadly disease—cancer.

Medical researchers have already found that pellets of gold, or liquids containing specks of gold, can destroy cancerous cells in such parts of the body as the prostate gland and the ovaries.

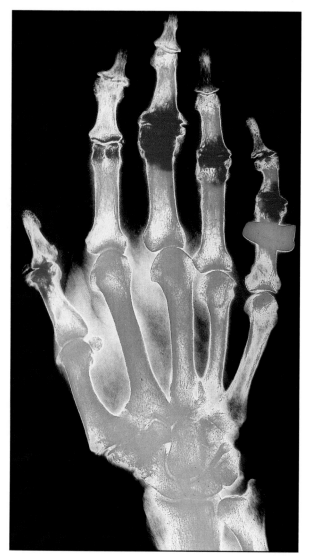

This X-ray image shows a hand affected by the disease arthritis. The red areas are swellings caused by arthritis. Creams that contain gold are used to treat arthritis.

This acupuncturist is using goldplated needles, which are especially safe to use as gold is not poisonous.

Researchers sometimes inject specks of gold into parts of the body to see how well the parts are working. Since gold is dense, traces of gold inside body tissue show up well on electron-microscope images— pictures that show objects in minute detail.

Gold tests

Gold combined with DNA is already under trial as a drug to fight HIV infections. Soon, gold may also be used to check for the scraps of DNA that are telltale signs of certain diseases. Specks of gold only one half of a millionth of an inch (13 millionths of a millimeter) in diameter look ruby red when they are mixed with water. When they are brought near to DNA, the specks clump together and become pinkish gray. Scientists hope to use color changes of gold specks to check for DNA in minutes.

DID YOU KNOW?

LIFESAVING COMBINATION
DNA is a complex chemical found in the cells of living things, and it helps to determine how each individual living thing grows. Scientists are combining gold with the DNA found in the cells of humans. They hope to use this combination of gold and DNA in drugs that can attack HIV, the virus that causes the deadly disease AIDS.

A thin coating of gold is applied to a medical specimen before it is put under an electron microscope to be examined.

Measuring gold

HALLMARKS

Hallmarks—used to guarantee the quality of gold articles—are usually made up of four parts:
- a symbol or initials that identify the maker or designer
- a number (usually a value in points) that indicates the purity
- a symbol that identifies the place where the gold was assayed (had its purity tested)
- a code letter that indicates the year of manufacture.

Gold is expensive, so traders measure it out very carefully. People who buy gold also need to ensure that they get exactly what they pay for. Over the years, several systems have been devised to measure gold and govern its quality.

As gold is usually mixed with other metals, people have developed ways to measure its purity. Jewelers measure the purity of a gold object in karats. This tells them how many parts per 24 are made of gold. Chemists prefer to measure gold purity in fineness. This tells them how many parts per thousand are made of gold. Pure gold is 24-karat and has a fineness of 1000. A material made of 50 percent gold is 12-karat and has a fineness of 500. The same system is used in Europe, where a 12-karat ring would be valued at 500 points, an 18-karat ring at 750 points, and so on.

The marks on this gold bar tell you that its weight is 500 grams and that it has a fineness of 999.9 points. That means it is 99.99 percent pure.

DID YOU KNOW?

SIGNS OF QUALITY

In Britain, where the hallmark system for certifying the quality of gold was first adopted, there are four Assay Offices. Each has its own identifying symbol, which appears on the hallmarked object along with other information. Birmingham, London, and Sheffield, England, are represented respectively by an anchor, a leopard, and a rose, and Edinburgh, in Scotland, by a castle.

Gold objects are ususally hallmarked to say how pure the gold is and when and where its purity was tested.

To stop people passing off other metals as gold, the British government introduced hallmarks around 600 years ago. Still in use today, a hallmark is a sign on a gold object that guarantees it is made of gold. The hallmark also tells you when the object was made and where it came from. In many countries it is illegal to sell gold objects without a hallmark that guarantees their quality.

A weighty problem

Scientists weigh gold, like any other substance, in kilograms (one kilogram equals 2.2 pounds). But, traditionally, goldsmiths, jewelers, assayers, and others in the gold business have weighed gold in units called "troy ounces," which weigh a little more than standard ounces. One troy ounce equals 1.097 standard ounces, or 31.10 grams.

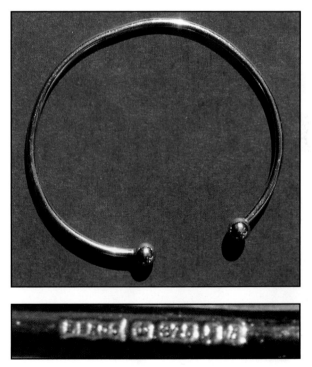

This magnified hallmark, which is stamped on the inside of the bracelet shown above, serves as a guarantee of the quality of the gold it is made from.

Periodic table

Everything in the universe is made from combinations of substances called elements. Elements are the building blocks of matter. They are made of tiny atoms, which are much too small to see.

The character of an atom depends on how many even tinier particles called protons there are in its center, or nucleus. An element's atomic number is the same as the number of protons.

Scientists have found around 110 different elements. About 90 elements occur naturally on Earth. The rest have been made in experiments.

All these elements are set out on a chart called the periodic table. This lists all the elements in order according to their atomic number.

The elements at the left of the table are metals. Those at the right are nonmetals. Between the metals and the nonmetals are the metalloids, which sometimes act like metals and sometimes like nonmetals.

- On the left of the table are the alkali metals. These elements have just one electron in their outer shells.

- On the right of the periodic table are the noble gases. These elements have full outer shells.

- Elements in the same group have the same number of electrons in their outer shells.

- Elements get more reactive as you go down a group.

- The number of electrons orbiting the nucleus increases down each group.

- The transition metals are in the middle of the table, between Groups II and III.

Group I

Group II

Transition metals

1 H Hydrogen 1								
3 Li Lithium 7	4 Be Beryllium 9							
11 Na Sodium 23	12 Mg Magnesium 24							
19 K Potassium 39	20 Ca Calcium 40	21 Sc Scandium 45	22 Ti Titanium 48	23 V Vanadium 51	24 Cr Chromium 52	25 Mn Manganese 55	26 Fe Iron 56	27 Co Cobalt 59
37 Rb Rubidium 85	38 Sr Strontium 88	39 Y Yttrium 89	40 Zr Zirconium 91	41 Nb Niobium 93	42 Mo Molybdenum 96	43 Tc Technetium (98)	44 Ru Ruthenium 101	45 Rh Rhodium 103
55 Cs Cesium 133	56 Ba Barium 137	71 Lu Lutetium 175	72 Hf Hafnium 179	73 Ta Tantalum 181	74 W Tungsten 184	75 Re Rhenium 186	76 Os Osmium 190	77 Ir Iridium 192
87 Fr Francium 223	88 Ra Radium 226	103 Lr Lawrencium (260)	104 Unq Unnilquadium (261)	105 Unp Unnilpentium (262)	106 Unh Unnilhexium (263)	107 Uns Unnilseptium (?)	108 Uno Unniloctium (?)	109 Une Unnilennium (?)

Lanthanide elements

Actinide elements

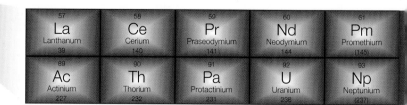

| 57
La
Lanthanum
39 | 58
Ce
Cerium
140 | 59
Pr
Praseodymium
141 | 60
Nd
Neodymium
144 | 61
Pm
Promethium
(145) |
| 89
Ac
Actinium
227 | 90
Th
Thorium
232 | 91
Pa
Protactinium
231 | 92
U
Uranium
238 | 93
Np
Neptunium
(237) |

The horizontal rows are called periods. As you go across a period, the atomic number increases by one from each element to the next. The vertical columns are called groups. Elements get heavier as you go down a group. All the elements in a group have the same number of electrons in their outer shells. This means they react in similar ways.

The transition metals fall between Groups II and III. Their electron shells fill up in an unusual way. The lanthanide elements and the actinide elements are set apart from the main table to make it easier to read. All the lanthanide elements and the actinide elements are quite rare.

Gold in the table

Gold has atomic number 79, so it has 79 protons in its nucleus. It is one of the heaviest of the group of elements termed transition metals.

Like many metals, gold is shiny and a good conductor of electricity and heat. Unlike most metals, it is very unreactive, which is why it is so highly prized.

Metals

Metalloids (semimetals)

Nonmetals

79	Atomic (proton) number
Au	Symbol
Gold	Name
197	Atomic mass

Group VIII

Group III	Group IV	Group V	Group VI	Group VII	2 He Helium 4
5 B Boron 11	6 C Carbon 12	7 N Nitrogen 14	8 O Oxygen 16	9 F Fluorine 19	10 Ne Neon 20
13 Al Aluminum 27	14 Si Silicon 28	15 P Phosphorus 31	16 S Sulfur 32	17 Cl Chlorine 35	18 Ar Argon 40

28 Ni Nickel 59	29 Cu Copper 64	30 Zn Zinc 65	31 Ga Gallium 70	32 Ge Germanium 73	33 As Arsenic 75	34 Se Selenium 79	35 Br Bromine 80	36 Kr Krypton 84
46 Pd Palladium 106	47 Ag Silver 108	48 Cd Cadmium 112	49 In Indium 115	50 Sn Tin 119	51 Sb Antimony 122	52 Te Tellurium 128	53 I Iodine 127	54 Xe Xenon 131
78 Pt Platinum 195	79 Au Gold 197	80 Hg Mercury 201	81 Tl Thallium 204	82 Pb Lead 207	83 Bi Bismuth 209	84 Po Polonium (209)	85 At Astatine (210)	86 Rn Radon (222)

| 62 Sm Samarium 150 | 63 Eu Europium 152 | 64 Gd Gadolinium 157 | 65 Tb Terbium 159 | 66 Dy Dysprosium 163 | 67 Ho Holmium 165 | 68 Er Erbium 167 | 69 Tm Thulium 169 | 70 Yb Ytterbium 173 |
| 94 Pu Plutonium (244) | 95 Am Americium (243) | 96 Cm Curium (247) | 97 Bk Berkelium (247) | 98 Cf Californium (251) | 99 Es Einsteinium (252) | 100 Fm Fermium (257) | 101 Md Mendelevium (258) | 102 No Nobelium (259) |

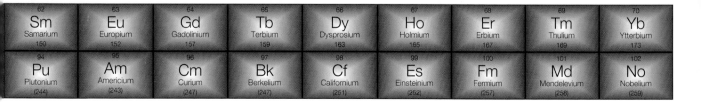

Chemical reactions

The rover vehicle from the Pathfinder *mission. This mission relied on gold circuitry to make sure the equipment worked far from home.*

Chemical reactions are going on around us all the time. Some reactions involve just two substances; others many more. But whenever a reaction takes place, at least one substance is changed.

In a chemical reaction, the atoms stay the same. But they join up in different combinations to form new molecules.

Gold is unusual in that it is so very unreactive. Unlike most metals, it does not react with pure acids to form salts, and it is also immune to the action of strong alkaline solutions. In part, gold is so unreactive because it is so dense. Its atoms are packed so closely together that atoms of other elements find it difficult to force their way between them to form new chemical bonds. So, in gold, the bonds that exist between its own atoms are stronger than those it forms with other atoms.

Under certain conditions, gold *will* form compounds. But these compounds are not very stable and are easily changed back (or "reduced") to the pure metal again.

A more stable way of getting gold to combine with other elements is in the form of an alloy. Alloys of gold—such as pink gold and white gold—are combinations of gold with another metal, often several other metals.

Glossary

alchemist: An early chemist who tried to turn ordinary metals into gold.

alloy: A mixture of a metal with another element, often another metal.

aqua regia: Latin for "royal water." A mixture of three parts nitric acid to one part hydrochloric acid, it is one of the few chemicals that can dissolve pure gold.

atom: The smallest amount of an element that has all the properties of that element. Each atom is less than a millionth of a millimeter in diameter.

atomic number: The number of protons in an atom. A proton is a tiny particle found inside the nucleus of an atom.

bullion: Large ingots of gold, usually held in a secure vault.

casting: Pouring molten metal into a mold, then letting it set into a solid object.

compound: A substance made of atoms of more than one element. Water is a compound of hydrogen and oxygen.

conductor: A substance that lets electricity or heat flow through it easily.

ductile: A ductile material, such as gold, is one that can be stretched easily.

electroplating: The process of using electricity to put a thin layer of one metal on top of another.

element: A substance made of only one type of atom. Gold is one of the elements.

fineness: A measure of the purity of gold. It tells you how many parts per thousand of a gold object are pure gold.

gold leaf: Sheets of gold that are less than a thousandth of a millimeter thick.

goldsmith: Someone who specializes in making things from gold.

hallmark: A marking stamped on a gold (or silver) object, verifying it as genuine.

infrared: Radiation similar to visible light, but invisible to the naked eye. The hotter an object is, the more infrared it gives off.

ingot: A solid bar of any metal, but generally applied to precious metals.

karat: A measure of the purity of a gold object. This tells you how many parts out of 24 of the object are made of gold.

luster: The shininess of most pure metals.

malleable: Malleable materials, such as gold, can be easily hammered into shapes.

metal: An element on the left of the periodic table.

mineral: A compound or element as it is found in its natural form on Earth.

periodic table: A chart of the elements set out in order of their atomic numbers.

placer deposits: Loose chunks of gold in sand or gravel.

rolled gold: A material made of gold that is at least 10 karat, pressed over a much cheaper metal, such as nickel or lead.

troy ounce: A traditional measure of the weight of gold. One troy ounce equals 1.097 ordinary ounces or 31.10 grams.

Index